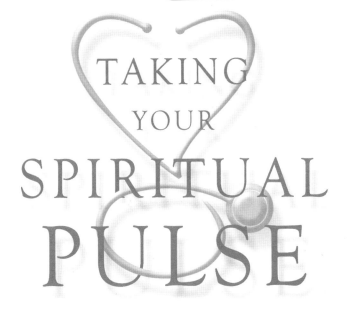

TAKING
YOUR
SPIRITUAL
PULSE

REACH THE PEAK OF SPIRITUAL FITNESS

TAKING YOUR SPIRITUAL PULSE

REACH THE PEAK OF SPIRITUAL FITNESS

CLAIRE MUSTERS

Advancing the Ministries of the Gospel

AMG *Publishers*

God's Word to you is our highest calling.

First published in 2003 by
AMG Publishers
6815 Shallowford Road
Chattanooga, TN 37421

ISBN 0-89957-377-0

This book was conceived,
designed, and produced by

 THE PALM PRESS

The Old Candlemakers
West Street, Lewes
East Sussex BN7 2NZ, U.K.

Creative Director: Peter Bridgewater
Publisher: Sophie Collins
Editorial Director: Steve Luck
Designer: Andrew Milne
Project Editor: Caroline Earle

Printed in China

CONTENTS

Introduction

ABOVE **Get into the habit of taking regular time out to examine where you are spiritually.**

Have you ever tried to give yourself a spiritual checkup? Or does the notion seem totally alien to you? If so, are you the sort of person who would never go near a doctor or a health clinic until you were rushed into hospital on a stretcher? Although assessing your spiritual health can be a sobering experience, remember that you aren't going to be perfect until you reach heaven. Every single Christian would benefit from a regular spiritual checkup. As you undertake yours, decide from the outset that you will look to God to heal your spiritual ailments once you've pinpointed what they are.

Make sure you don't risk your spiritual health! The best approach to healthcare is early diagnosis, which allows problems to be put right before they get worse. This little book helps you to diagnose any problems in your spiritual life. Take an accurate reading of your current level of spiritual fitness simply by answering the series of questions that are provided at the start. It will cost you nothing but the price of this book—but it will require a lot of honesty.

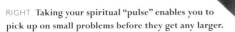
RIGHT **Taking your spiritual "pulse" enables you to pick up on small problems before they get any larger.**

As you identify problems, there is help in dealing with them before they grow and spread. In the following pages you will find a complete set of guidelines to help you attain a healthy spiritual condition—as well as advice on how to keep in shape once you are there. All you need now is a determination to get spiritually fit and an openness to change habits and lifestyles where you need to. Just remember that you aren't doing this alone.

Every Christian is called to become more like Christ, and this involves working on those areas of your life that hinder the process. Jesus is your "personal trainer"—so let Him speak to you through these pages. Take His advice and you can be assured that your spirit will become fitter, happier, and healthier.

LEFT **Allowing Jesus to guide your spiritual health will make you a much happier, whole person.**

Why do you need a spiritual checkup?

In this day and age a lot of emphasis is placed on physical health—some people spend hours exercising their body every week—and yet spiritual health is largely ignored. This is crazy, because humans are fundamentally spiritual beings: God made us that way. Everyone has a built-in need to connect with God, so when they are not doing so it feels as though something is missing. That is why it is so important to assess your spiritual life on a regular basis.

TAKING YOUR SPIRITUAL PULSE

ASSESSING YOUR SPIRITUAL HEALTH

Most people keep a close eye on their physical health and cut out fat or sugar if they find they have gained too much weight. It's also important to assess honestly whether your spiritual life is sick or healthy. It is not so different from your physical body in the sense that you need to look after it to ensure it stays in shape.

Exercise and dieting take discipline—and so does looking after your spirit. You won't automatically wake up one day, decide to ensure your spirit is healthy, and find it's happened by the end of the day! As the apostle Paul says, life is a race and things take time, but you have your whole life to work at it.

As a Christian you need to realize that your life on earth is your training for eternal life—so don't waste it! You are running toward your eternal rewards, and daily disciplines such as prayer and Bible study will enable you to keep running. You must train diligently in order to be able to keep your pace up.

LEFT **Watching your diet is vital for physical health. The same applies to spiritual fitness. Ensure that you only take in what is good for you.**

RIGHT **Take time out to assess whether you are "shaping up" spiritually.**

"Do you not know that in a race all the runners run, but only one gets the prize? Run in such a way as to get the prize. Everyone who competes in the games goes into strict training. They do it to get a crown that will not last; but we do it to get a crown that will last for ever." 1 Corinthians 9: 24–25

ASK YOURSELF

- **Do I sometimes wonder if there really is a God?**

- **Do I sometimes wonder if I'm even a Christian?**

- **Do I wonder if God is always good?**

- **Do I make time every day for reading and studying the Bible?**

- **When did I last have a true experience of worship?**

- **Do I ever speak critically of the church, the family of God?**

- **Do I realize that worship of God is the highest activity I'm capable of?**

If you have read the questions in the box and now feel like a spiritual couch potato, take heart—everyone has their

doubts and difficulties at times and God doesn't expect you to be perfect this side of heaven! What He does want from you, though, is total commitment and surrender to Him.

Many people encounter difficulties in their spiritual lives. Although they've acknowledged they believe in Him and want Him to take His rightful place within their hearts, they then spend a lot of their time fighting it, trying to take back control. Are you like that?

It's important to learn that your spiritual life will be at its healthiest, and you will be at your happiest, when you allow God to have His way. Such surrender shouldn't be seen in a negative light—it is a positive decision that provides the only way to find genuine freedom and peace.

You may have read this far and still feel that there is nothing wrong with your spiritual life. If so, answer the following questions honestly:

(?) **Have I been stuck in a spiritual rut recently?**

(?) **Did I go through the whole day today without thinking about God?**

(?) **Am I happy to be a Christian just when I'm at church?**

(?) **Did I purposefully bypass an opportunity to talk about my faith today?**

(?) **Is there one particular sin in my life that I am not prepared to give up on any account?**

LEFT **Discipline may seem tough to start with, but it will help you to be healthier and freer, too.**

If you can answer yes to any or all of these questions, then perhaps, this will convince you that you need a spiritual checkup—as we all do. It isn't until you can identify the areas of your life that need the most attention that you can figure out what work needs to be done. Then you can take action to keep yourself spiritually fit day by day.

"Let us fix our eyes on Jesus, the author and perfector of our faith...Consider him who endured such opposition from sinful men, so that you will not grow weary and lose heart."
Hebrews 12: 2–3a

GETTING STARTED

You should begin the process slowly and be realistic. There is no point in setting goals that are far too difficult—that will just disappoint you before you've even got going. If you'd never tried running to keep fit before, you wouldn't tackle a five-mile run on the first day, would you? You'd work up to it, train by walking, jogging, and then running a little farther each day. The same approach is needed here. The most important thing is to persevere and keep at it. Continue at whatever pace you feel able, and you will see your spiritual life transformed.

Whenever you feel as though it is too difficult, just remember what Jesus did for you! And be aware that you don't have to do it all by yourself, using your own strength—God is with you all the way.

LEFT **Make sure that you start slowly, with small, achievable changes. Don't try to "run" without walking and jogging first...**

TAKING YOUR SPIRITUAL PULSE

Your spiritual checkup

In this section it is important to take the time to assess your life honestly. Your spiritual life shouldn't be separate from the rest of your life—it should pervade every part of you. The questions that you will find on the next few pages are designed to make you think about how you act in various situations and with different people.

spiritual

The questions below have been organized into groups of ten, each concentrating on a particular part of life, such as relationships, work, or witnessing. It is within these areas that the state of your spiritual health is truly revealed and tested. For example, perhaps you make a real effort to watch what you say at work to be a good witness, but back at home things are very different!

Think carefully about the questions and check yes or no for each one. When you have finished the checkup and added up your score (see page 23) you will have an indication of how fit you are in each area of your spiritual life.

GENERAL LIFESTYLE

	YES	NO
Am I known as a Christian?	O	O
Is my behavior better than that of nonbeliever friends?	O	O
Do people look at me and see Christ?	O	O
Would I be happy inviting friends along to my church?	O	O
Do I view my home and everything in it as belonging to God?	O	O
Do I involve God in my everyday life?	O	O
Am I generally thankful to God for my day-to-day circumstances?	O	O
Am I strictly honest?	O	O
Do I truly think of everyone around me as my equal?	O	O
Do I look after my body, and avoid overeating, liquor, and tobacco?	O	O

checkup

RELATIONSHIPS

	YES	NO
Do those who know me best believe in and trust me the most?	○	○
Is my behavior at home the same as it is outside of it?	○	○
Do I thank God for those who help me every day?	○	○
Do I even realize that people are helping me?	○	○
Have I encouraged my spouse/best friend/children today?	○	○
Am I friendly and happy even when I'm tired?	○	○
Could I happily account for my alone times to my spouse/best friend?	○	○
And for my every thought?	○	○
Do I put my spouse/family/friends before myself?	○	○
Am I the first to seek reconciliation after a disagreement?	○	○

LEFT **You may want to write your answers on a separate piece of paper, so you can reuse the checkup as often as necessary.**

spiritual

WORK

	YES	NO
Am I easy to work with?	O	O
Do I do more than my fair share quietly, without looking for praise?	O	O
Do I really love the people I work with?	O	O
Is doing God's will more important to me than getting a promotion?	O	O
Am I content with my job or am I always looking to move on?	O	O
Am I happy when others are praised, even if I am overlooked?	O	O
Do I stick up for people if they are unfairly treated at work?	O	O
Am I willing to take my praise from God alone?	O	O
Do I think of my job as an opportunity to advance God's kingdom?	O	O
Do I try and act as peacemaker when meetings or other situations turn hostile?	O	O

checkup

MONEY

	YES	NO
Do I give as much to those who can't give back as to those who can?	○	○
Do I try to avoid debt?	○	○
Do I view my income as being God's, rather than my own?	○	○
Do I give to those in need?	○	○
Do I tithe from my monthly income?	○	○
If not, do I think I should?	○	○
Can I say, honestly, that money is not something I run after?	○	○
Am I content with my income?	○	○
If I receive an unexpected gift, do I tithe part of it?	○	○
Do I put family and friends' material needs before my own?	○	○

spiritual

TAKING YOUR SPIRITUAL PULSE

BASIC BEHAVIOR

	YES	NO
Have I refrained from swearing in the last week?	○	○
From losing my temper?	○	○
From telling a dirty joke?	○	○
Am I the same person when I'm not with my partner/family as I am when I am with them?	○	○
Do I watch what I think about rather than letting my mind wander?	○	○
Do I watch what I say?	○	○
Have I made a conscious effort not to lie this week?	○	○
Would others describe me as someone who never criticizes others behind their backs?	○	○
Do I quickly deal with any jealousy/hurt/anger I feel when it occurs?	○	○
Am I happy being myself, without feeling the need to conform?	○	○

20

checkup

WITNESSING

	YES	NO
Am I happy with the concept of sharing my faith?	O	O
Have I told someone I'm a Christian in the last week?	O	O
Do I believe God can use me to reach people?	O	O
Have I ever led anyone to Christ?	O	O
Do I view my friendships with nonbelievers as opportunities for evangelism?	O	O
Do I provide practical help to the elderly, ill, and lonely who live in my neighborhood?	O	O
Do I feel love for people I don't know, simply for themselves?	O	O
Do I truly believe that I am one of God's ambassadors?	O	O
Do I think that people have seen the love of Jesus through the way I've interacted with them this week?	O	O
Am I a witness through my actions as well as my words?	O	O

spiritual

PRAYER

	YES	NO
Did I spend time talking to God today?	○	○
Do I ever pray with those I love best?	○	○
Do I enjoy praying?	○	○
Do I pray for God's will to be done, rather than constantly telling Him what I want?	○	○
Do I ever pray for those around me, both my friends and my enemies?	○	○
Do I ever spend time listening for God's response when I pray?	○	○
Do I look forward to church prayer meetings?	○	○
Do I acknowledge God by saying grace before meals, whether I'm with others or not?	○	○
Have I prayed in the last week for world leaders, including those who are viewed as enemies?	○	○
Do I expect God to answer my prayers?	○	○

checkup

Now you have finished working through the questions, simply add up the number of yes's and no's you have under each heading. If you have six or more yes's in a section then well done—you are looking after and developing that particular side of your spiritual health effectively. Keep up the good work!

Now look at the areas where you scored five or less—these are the places where you seriously need to concentrate on working out and shaping up!

This quick and easy "test" helps you to assess where you are just now. As you work on the areas that were highlighted as needing attention, you will find that your score will eventually change. Try redoing the test in a few months' time and it might help you pinpoint a different area that needs some work.

RESULTS (6+ YES'S)

	YES	NO
Lifestyle	○	○
Relationships	○	○
Work	○	○
Money	○	○
Behavior	○	○
Witnessing	○	○
Prayer	○	○

RIGHT **So how did you measure up? Keep your answers safe so that you can compare scores when you do the test again.**

10 ways to improve your spiritual life

This section provides some basic principles that will help you to improve your spiritual life. Your life as a Christian will always be challenging—it would be dull if it wasn't—but there are some simple steps that you can take to ensure that your spiritual life is on the right track. These will, at times, involve some life-changing decisions. As you persevere they will help you to grow spiritually and achieve a breakthrough in the areas of your life that you find the most difficult to open up to God. Work through these pages at your own pace—the important thing is to try to implement what you read and learn.

I. HAVE A REGULAR DEVOTIONAL TIME

*A*n athlete in training puts together a daily program in order to keep *fit, and you should use a similar approach in your spiritual life. The discipline of spending regular time with God is essential because it is then, when you are concentrating on Him. It is then that your faith can grow. During such times He can also reveal what He wants to change in you to make you more like Jesus.*

ABOVE **Find a place where you can spend uninterrupted time with God.**

WHAT IS A DEVOTIONAL TIME?

It may sound very pious and proper, but a devotional time is simply a portion of your day that you set aside to be with God. During this time you can read the Bible, pray, and listen to what He wants to say to you. The purpose is very simple—to get to know God better. You can't become like Him if you don't know much about Him!

Being a Christian is all about being in a relationship with God. You need to understand more about Him and the more you learn the more you will want to learn. This makes the whole process easier. Even if it feels like a discipline at first, it will soon become a precious part of your day that you look forward to.

GETTING STARTED

If you have never tried having a devotional time, please don't go into the process thinking that it is a necessary chore that has to be done each day to make you a "good" Christian. It certainly isn't about the amount of time spent, but about the quality of time. God wants to be your friend. It will hurt Him if you simply whizz through a daily reading, think you've done your bit, and then ignore Him for the rest of the day. On the other hand, don't feel you have to launch into an hour-long devotion immediately. Start small, and work up. Try starting with just five or ten minutes and, after a week or two, extend the time-frame slightly. Keep building on it.

It can be extremely helpful to schedule your devotional time for first thing in the morning. This ensures that you've put God first (although the important thing is to set aside regular devotional time, whatever part of the day it is). You can also then invite Him to be with you throughout the day and ask Him what His specific purposes are for you that day.

ABOVE **Early morning is often a good time to read your Bible and pray.**

BELOW **Short, daily exercise is the best way to build up stamina. The same is true for your devotional time.**

Some Christians find that when they are very busy, their devotional time is swallowed up by other commitments. They may get to the end of the day, fall into bed, and realize that they haven't had a chance to stop and talk to God at all. This is another reason why it is helpful to get into the habit of spending time with Him in the morning. That might mean setting your alarm a half hour earlier when you have a busy day ahead. It makes it much more likely that you will continue to speak to God throughout the day if you have made contact as soon as you wake up. And putting God first like this usually results in a more successful day, however much there is to get done (see Balancing Your Time, pages 86–87).

27

TOP
TIP

Choose and memorize a Bible verse this week.

READING THE BIBLE

The Bible is like medicine for your soul. God has provided guidelines and scenarios within it that are as relevant to Christians today as they were when it was first written. He has given it as a gift so, instead of wondering why you don't feel any input from Him in your life, you should look to see what He has said within its pages.

To help you understand the Bible more deeply, and learn how to apply it to your own life, you could try using teaching notes—there are plenty that are easily available.

ABOVE **Try to set aside time to really concentrate on reading a longer passage in the Bible without any distractions.**

Learning more about His word will equip you with the correct tools required for everyday living and for responding in a godly way to all kinds of situations. You can use the Bible as your measuring stick, because it reveals God's standards. When you read it, it will reassure you of your salvation, encourage you in your daily life, strengthen you in your faith, and bring correction where it is needed.

"All scripture is God-breathed and useful for teaching, rebuking, correcting, and training in righteousness, so that the man of God may be thoroughly equipped for every good work." 2 Timothy 3: 16–17

TALKING TO GOD

Being a Christian is all about having a relationship with God, so it is important to spend time listening and talking to Him. That is what praying is—enjoying a conversation with a friend. When you learn to talk and listen to God, you are entering into a vital, dynamic part of your relationship with Him—one that will help you grow.

What God actually wants you to do is to "pray continually" (*I Thessalonians 5: 17*). This doesn't mean that you have to be locked away in a small room by yourself all day—He just wants you to keep in touch with Him throughout the day and ask His advice when making decisions. In this way, He can be a part of your life at all times. When you call on Him in prayer He will begin to reveal more of Himself to you.

HEALTH CHECKLIST

☺ *Have I spent time with God today?*

☺ *If so, was it "quality time" I enjoyed or was I simply watching the clock until I felt I'd done enough?*

BELOW **You can talk to God at any time, wherever you are—even when you are traveling to work.**

2. ATTEND CHURCH

Exercise classes exist because people find it easier to sustain motivation when they are surrounded by like-minded people with the same goal. That is why being part of a church is so important—as a Christian you need the support and encouragement of others in order to maintain the impetus to work on your spiritual fitness.

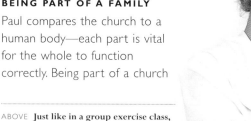

Going to church each Sunday isn't something that you should do out of a sense of duty. God chose to express His love through the church—He refers to it as "the bride of Christ." The way the church functions should reveal this fact to the world. When you reflect on how important the church is to God, don't you want to be a part of it?

BEING PART OF A FAMILY

Paul compares the church to a human body—each part is vital for the whole to function correctly. Being part of a church helps you to discover the particular gifts God has given you (*see page 91*) and learn what role He wants you to play within that community. The church is a family and within it you will learn how to work with many different types of people.

ABOVE **Just like in a group exercise class, in church there will be people who will keep you motivated as a Christian.**

You may not be naturally drawn to some of the people you will encounter, but you will have a common purpose and belief that unites you.

It is important to realize that being part of the same church will not automatically mean you agree on everything, but you should learn to work together in love in spite of your differences. You can also gain a lot from the many different types and age groups of people that you will encounter. Nowhere else in society will you receive the same depth of experience as belonging to a group with such wide variety in its membership.

> *"God has arranged the parts in the body, every one of them, just as he wanted them to be. If they were all one part, where would the body be? As it is, there are many parts, but one body."*
> *1 Corinthians 12: 18–20*

There is something powerful about worshipping in a collective group of people—it is a source of encouragement and adds an extra dimension to your spiritual life. Hearing God's Word preached and explained will feed you and encourage you in your faith. God has provided you with teachers and preachers within your local church. It would be foolish not to take advantage of the opportunity!

OP ⏵

is Sunday, roduce yourself to neone you've ver spoken to ore.

HEALTH CHECKLIST

- ☺ *Do I regularly attend church or am I sporadic in my approach?*

- ☺ *Do I see church as a chore or do I look forward to it?*

- ☺ *Have I built strong relationships with people in my church, or do I avoid getting to know anyone better?*

LEFT Belonging to a church means that you are part of God's family, made up of all age groups.

31

3. GET RID OF DISTRACTIONS AND TEMPTATIONS

In your effort to get spiritually fit, you will encounter things that distract your attention or tempt you away from your goal.
It's the same as if you were on a diet that cut out all sugary foods and then you found, perhaps after a day or two, that you were craving a bar of chocolate.

A distraction is anything that takes your focus away from God. It may not be bad in itself, but if it takes too much of your attention it could become an idol, as it begins to take the place of God. For instance, it might be that you look forward to getting home after a hard day's work, kicking off your shoes, and sitting in front of the television with a soft drink.

ABOVE **Be honest—what is it that tempts your spiritual being in the same way as a cream cake can make your mouth water?**

Then all of a sudden you find the whole evening has gone by and all you've done is watch television. In this way, it has taken your evening and crowded out any time for God.

You need to learn to switch off distractions to concentrate on God—whether these include the television, computer games, or using the internet. You may need to give up certain things, at least for a while, if they are hindering you.

BELOW It is important to be focused when you are trying to cut out distractions and stay away from temptations.

If this sounds too difficult or harsh, listen to what Jesus said: "If your eye causes you to sin, gouge it out and throw it away. It is better for you to enter life with one eye than to have two eyes and be thrown into the fire of hell." (*Matthew 18: 9*). When you think with an eternal perspective, giving up your favorite television program or using the computer for a while doesn't seem that big a deal!

Once you have broken the habit, and the hold it had over you, you may find you can once again enjoy that favorite pastime, without it taking over. However, if you find yourself slipping back into letting it take up too much of your time, and it means you take your focus off God once more, then you will need to give it up for good. This is just the same as giving up a certain food if it caused you to become sick.

LEFT At times you may need to cut out things that you enjoy, such as watching TV, in order to concentrate more on God.

TAKING YOUR SPIRITUAL PULSE

ABOVE **When facing temptation there are two choices—you** *can* **take the right path.**

OVERCOMING TEMPTATION

Everyone is tempted at times— being a Christian doesn't mean you are automatically immune from this. Temptation is not a sin in itself; after all, Jesus himself was tempted. The crucial part is that He didn't give in to it and you don't have to either.

If you do struggle with temptation, remember that it doesn't mean that there is something intrinsically wrong with you. Every Christian faces temptation. However, it may be that you find one particular temptation recurs again and again and you keep giving in to it. While temptation may seem like a disease, it is not fatal!

You must admit to yourself that you have a problem. Realize that others have managed to overcome it, and that God has given you everything you need to do so. The blood of Jesus ultimately conquered all the problems and issues that you struggle with. His sacrifice has a redeeming quality and can transform your spiritual life if you pray and ask for His help. It would be useful to ask a trustworthy friend to help you. You also need to make a conscious decision to do what is right, and avoid any situation that you know will put the temptation directly in your path.

During the process of honestly assessing your spiritual life, you may come to realize that you don't actually want to overcome a particular temptation. If this is the case, you need to understand how it is stifling your spiritual life—that it is truly a matter of life or death: "For if you live according to the sinful nature, you will die;

"No temptation has seized you except what is common to man. And God is faithful; he will not let you be tempted beyond what you can bear. But when you are tempted, he will also provide a way out so that you can stand up under it."
1 Corinthians 10: 12–13

34

but if by the Spirit you put to death the misdeeds of the body, you will live." (*Romans 8: 13*).

Of course, the devil will pick something to which he knows you are susceptible. Put simply, temptation just wouldn't be tempting if it didn't appear desirable. Open your eyes, and think about where this temptation could lead.

HEALTH CHECKLIST

- *What is it that fills up all of my free time?*

- *Would I be willing to give it up, at least for a while, in order to focus more on my spiritual life?*

- *Is there something that regularly tempts me that I give in to every time?*

TOP TIP

If you are really struggling with a particular temptation, get up the courage this week to ask a friend to support you as you work at overcoming it.

4. JOIN A SMALL GROUP

You were not designed to be an island—everyone needs interaction with other people. You will find that in your Christian journey you can't be self-sufficient. Without Christian fellowship your spiritual life will simply become dry. If you take a piece of coal out of a blazing fire and leave it on its own, it goes out very quickly. You don't want to be like that piece of coal, do you?

ABOVE **You'll be unable to keep up momentum in your spiritual life if you choose to go it alone rather than spending time with other Christians.**

Although it is very important to be part of a church, it is often quite difficult to cultivate close friendships in such a large group. That's why many churches have smaller group meetings during the week, in which individuals come together to support each other and learn from one another. Such small groups are excellent places to enjoy healthy discussion and debate. Perhaps they will discuss something that was said in a Sunday sermon and answer any questions people have.

TO T

Be brave this we —do something you never done befo in your sm gro

> "...let us consider how we may spur one another on toward love and good deeds. Let us not give up meeting together...but let us encourage one another."
>
> Hebrews 10: 24–5

ABOVE **The members of a small group can help one another stay on track by supporting each other.**

Group meetings can often give you a fresh perspective. You will probably find that your small group has members from all walks of life and at different spiritual stages. You will be able to learn from some of them, while you teach and encourage others. This dynamic is an important aspect of the small group—it enables you to grow but also provides you with a sense of purpose because you are helping others. As a small group, you can work together at reaching out to your neighborhood by showing them God's love in practical ways (see Serve Others pages 48–49).

Such groups are safe places where you can voice your struggles and ask for prayer and practical help. They provide an environment in which you can step out and try something new. If you've never prayed out loud in front of a group, then the idea of doing it in church may petrify you (and you may not be offered that opportunity). The same may be true for testing a new spiritual gift (see page 91). In a loving, smaller environment you can feel more comfortable trying out new experiences and challenges.

In a small group, surrounded by people that you've taken the time to get to know, trust, and love, your spiritual life will be nurtured and you'll be encouraged to grow.

HEALTH CHECKLIST

☺ *Am I part of a small group?*

☺ *If so, how much do I participate?*

☺ *If not, would I consider being part of one?*

☺ *If not, why not?*

LEFT **In a small group you can learn and discuss new things together.**

5. CONFESS YOUR SINS

It can be all too easy to think that God automatically forgives you when you make a mistake. However, it is important to remember that His forgiveness is conditional on true repentance. He is a just and pure God, and therefore cannot welcome you with open arms while you are harboring a sin for which you haven't repented.

Allowing sin to remain unconfessed will make running your spiritual race much more difficult. You will find that it creates obstacles and hurdles that slow you down significantly and keep you from reaching God's presence. Get into the habit of mentally checking over your life each day to see which sins you have committed, and then openly confess them to God. Don't let pride stop you from enjoying His

ABOVE **Just as you wash your body to get rid of impurities, so you need to confess sins in order to be cleansed from them.**

"If we confess our sins, he is faithful and just and will forgive us our sins and purify us from all unrighteousness." 1 John 1: 9

fellowship. If you find the thought of saying sorry too difficult, think about everything that Jesus did for you, and that should bring you to an attitude of thankfulness and humility.

Daily repentance is a good way to keep yourself humble before God. It is not enough simply to say "sorry" and then continue to commit the same sin. True repentance involves a willingness to turn away from the sin. If that seems too hard, remember that God's grace will help you to achieve it.

You may have sinned against a friend and when you ask God to forgive you, He prompts you to ask your friend for forgiveness. In such circumstances you will need to swallow your pride. Don't be scared of your friend's reaction; if God has spoken to you about asking that friend for forgiveness then He may well have talked to the friend about forgiving you! Even if your friend finds it difficult to forgive you, you will know that you have obeyed God and will feel inner peace afterward.

HEALTH CHECKLIST

☺ *Have I let any sin go unrepented today?*

☺ *Is there any sin that I need to ask for forgiveness from my brother or sister?*

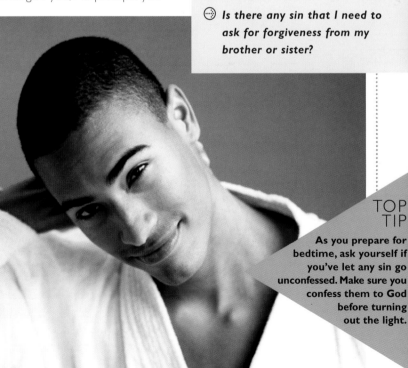

TOP TIP

As you prepare for bedtime, ask yourself if you've let any sin go unconfessed. Make sure you confess them to God before turning out the light.

TAKING YOUR SPIRITUAL PULSE

6. BE WISE WITH YOUR MONEY

It may be difficult to understand that every part of your life belongs to God—and that includes your money. Perhaps you were brought up to work hard to be financially secure. However, this could mean that you're focusing your attention on the wrong goal—money—rather than getting close to God. As a result you are turning and running in a direction that takes you farther away from Him.

ABOVE **God wants to be in charge of every area of your life, including your checkbook.**

The Bible says that you cannot serve both God and money. By running after money you're making it your idol. Ask yourself what you spend your money on each month. Take a close look at where your financial priorities lie and you may find you that you need to adjust your outgoings to reflect your spiritual values. If you discover that a big chunk of your income goes on entertainment and "extras" (anything you don't really need) while giving to the church is one of your lowest priorities, try reversing this order. God wants

LEFT **It can be tempting to buy lots of material things but take time to consider whether you really need them.**

RIGHT **Look after your money wisely, because God wants you to be a good steward of it. He also wants you to give a portion of it away.**

to see that you're willing to give everything to Him, even your hard-earned cash.

THE PRINCIPLE OF TITHING

Tithing is the act of giving your first fruits to God. In biblical times this was ten percent of an income, and many churches encourage this amount as a starting point when giving. The amount you give isn't fixed—for some, ten percent would be a struggle while for others that is nowhere near enough. The Bible says that: "If the willingness is there, the gift is acceptable according to what one has, not according to what he does not have." (*2 Corinthians 8: 12*).

TOP TIP

This month give ten percent of your income to your church and see how God blesses you.

The principle of tithing is helpful because it ensures, once again, that you are putting God first. It also demonstrates the fundamental belief that everything you have belongs to God.

"Bring a gift in proportion to the way the Lord your God has blessed you." Deuteronomy 16: 17

TAKING YOUR SPIRITUAL PULSE

LEFT AND BELOW **It doesn't matter how little you are able to give, so long as you give it willingly. God promises that if you sow you will also reap a harvest.**

If you don't have much money, it may seem like an odd suggestion that you give away a certain proportion of it before you take care of paying bills, buying food, and other necessities. However, giving out of a grateful heart produces blessings from God—and that's a promise! "Whoever sows sparingly will also reap sparingly, and whoever sows generously will also reap generously. Each man should give what he has decided in his heart to give, not reluctantly or under compulsion, for God loves a cheerful giver. And God is able to make all grace abound to you, so that in all things at all times, having all that you need, you will abound in every good work." (2 *Corinthians 9: 6–8*).

Giving reveals your faith in God for His provision. It shows Him that you believe and trust He will look after your needs when you put Him first.

IS HAVING MONEY WRONG?

Christians are often taught that money is evil, and the Bible is sometimes used to back this teaching up. In fact, the verse that is quoted says that: "The love of money is a root of all kinds of evil." (*I Timothy 6: 10*), not that money is evil in itself. It is simply true that it is very easy to become greedy and want more and more—and this can have disastrous effects on all other areas of your life. Honestly assess what you would be willing to do to get more money. What does this say about your character?

ABOVE **Many people work long hours for extra money, but this can mean that work takes priority over family and friends.**

It is important to realize that riches are only temporary and that God wants to teach you to be content with what you have. There are rich Christians in the world and there is nothing wrong with that. But the principle: "From everyone who has been given much, much will be demanded..." (*Luke 12: 48*), rings true in the area of finances, also—with money comes added responsibility. It can do a great deal of good, but only if you're willing to use it to help others. Just as you should be seeking God's will in every other area of your life, ask God what He wants you to do with your money.

HEALTH CHECKLIST

- *Do I tithe?*

- *If not, have I ever thought of doing so?*

- *What is my attitude toward money? Do I view it as evil? Have I made it my idol? Can I honestly say I understand that everything I have belongs to God?*

- *What do I actually need to live on?*

- *Do I yearn for things that aren't necessities?*

- *If I receive an unexpected sum of money, do I immediately think of what I could buy myself, or how I could use it to help others?*

TAKING YOUR SPIRITUAL PULSE

7. LEARN TO FORGIVE

*F*orgiving others as God has forgiven
you can sometimes be incredibly
difficult. However, if you allow a
grudge to develop against someone
who has hurt you, you will find that
it turns into bitterness. This, in turn,
will infect other areas of your Christian
life. Like a disease, it will spread
everywhere. Forgiveness is perhaps one
of the hardest principles to practice,
but it is crucial if you want to
grow as a Christian.

ABOVE **Just like a disease, unforgiveness
and bitterness will spread unless dealt
with quickly.**

FORGIVING SOMEONE WHO HAS HURT YOU

You might be hurt by your
enemies, or inadvertently
wounded by those closest to
you. Perhaps you are aware that
God has called you to forgive
those who hurt you, but all you
can manage to do is grit your
teeth and say "Okay, I forgive
you." Unfortunately that is not
enough for God—it must come
from the heart. Forgiving
somebody involves being able to
pray for God to bless them and
not bad-mouthing them.

This may seem unthinkable
to you because it's so painful
to pray for someone who has
hurt you. However, God clearly
commands you to "...bless those
who curse you, pray for those
who ill-treat you." (*Luke 6: 28*).
He points out that anyone can
love people who treat them
well: "If you do good to those
who are good to you, what
credit is that to you? Even
'sinners' do that." (*Luke 6: 33*).
That isn't all God wants—He
wants you to love and
forgive everyone.

If forgiving seems too hard, you should realize that the alternatives are much, much worse. You may instinctively want to get revenge, but by harboring such thoughts you are moving away from God, because He cannot tolerate such a sinful attitude. This means that you will end up losing the peace of being in close fellowship with Him. Jesus says: "But if you do not forgive men their sins, your Father will not forgive your sins." (*Matthew 6:15*).

How awful would it be for you to get what you truly deserve because you are blocking God's forgiveness? By refusing to forgive someone, you are setting yourself up as their judge and therefore you are trying to take the place of God. Be warned—by doing this you are trying to usurp God's authority and He won't tolerate that. It also implies that you haven't taken your own sin seriously enough and aren't totally grateful for the way God has forgiven you. You may be tempted to think that your sin isn't as bad as the sin that has been

RIGHT **If someone close to you hurts you, don't turn your back on him or her but reach out with forgiveness.**

ABOVE **If you choose to forgive, you will be freed from the hold that bitterness can have.**

committed against you, but again, you are playing judge and it will backfire on you. You are choosing to revert to the old law of "an eye for an eye." So when you demand justice, the devil will be ecstatic because it means he can demand that God judges you in exactly the same way.

"Do not judge, or you too will be judged. For in the same way you judge others, you will be judged, and with the measure you use, it will be measured to you."
Matthew 7: 1–2

Even if it seems selfish, you can choose to forgive for the simple reason that you don't want to be judged yourself. Put simply, forgiveness is vital for your own spiritual well-being. And by learning to practice it, even when it is seems too difficult, little by little you are becoming more like Jesus.

Jesus himself said that when you have enemies who seek to harm you, you should view yourself as blessed! Not only will God use the situation to form a more godly character in you, but you will also be storing up treasure in heaven: "Blessed are you when people insult you, persecute you, and falsely say all kinds of evil against you because of me. Rejoice and be glad, because great is your reward in heaven." (*Matthew 5: 11–12*).

FORGIVING YOURSELF

Often forgiving yourself can be a very hard thing. You may have worked on forgiving others and made great headway in that area, but still find it impossible to forgive yourself for the sins that keep tripping you up.

You need to start seeing yourself as God sees you, rather than staying mad at yourself for making that stupid mistake yet again. You've already seen that when you confess your sins He forgives you—that means He's

forgotten what you did so there is no need for you to remember. While you should acknowledge your mistakes, you then need to lay them down. It is a choice to forgive and forget past wrongs— and this applies to your own actions as well as the actions of others. This is a choice you need to make on a daily basis (*see also* When Guilt Lingers, pages 68–69).

(*see also* When Guilt Lingers, pages 68–69).

HEALTH CHECKLIST

- Is there someone I haven't forgiven for hurts caused in the past?

- Have I forgiven myself for past actions or am I remembering and dwelling on them?

LEFT **Knowing that you are forgiven by God and yourself will give you a sense of peace.**

TOP TIP

At the end of the day ask God to reveal if there's someone you haven't forgiven for the way they've treated you. Then consciously forgive them before going to sleep.

TAKING YOUR SPIRITUAL PULSE

8. SERVE OTHERS

Jesus came to earth to serve others rather than to be served. This is an important principle for you to put into practice yourself, because it is the way in which His love is shown to the world. As a Christian you have been chosen to minister to the "spiritually sick," through direct service to them or by demonstrating the way you love and serve those closest to you.

ABOVE **Serving can be as simple as fetching water for someone who is thirsty.**

TOP TIP

See if your neighbor needs some practical help this weekend.

You will have plenty of opportunities to practice serving—at home with your family, at work with colleagues, and with all the other people that you come across each day. Jesus showed His love by dying for us all. You may never be asked to lay down your life for a friend but sacrificial serving is all about giving of yourself without expecting anything in return.

Serving may involve being there for someone by listening to them, offering

LEFT **Put your Christian faith into practice by reaching out to those more in need than you are.**

> *"Do nothing out of selfish ambition or vain conceit, but in humility consider others better than yourselves. Each of you should look not only to your own interests, but also to the interests of others."*
> *Philippians 2: 3–4*

them a simple encouraging word, or helping them out in some practical way. It is about opening your eyes to see their needs, and then putting them first, before yourself.

WHO YOU ARE REALLY SERVING?

If the concept of giving up your time to help others is difficult to accept, remember that by doing so you're being obedient to God because he specifically commanded you to in the Bible. If you need a change of perspective on this, see *Matthew 25: 37–40*, where Jesus says, "...whatever you did for one of the least of these brothers of mine, you did for me." (verse 40). He is pointing out that whenever you serve someone here on earth, you're in fact serving your Father in heaven. That makes taking every opportunity to serve those around you seem much more important.

REACHING OUT TO YOUR NEIGHBORHOOD

You could put the principle of serving into practice by searching out any voluntary service you could do to help a disadvantaged group in your neighborhood. You will be surprised how much you get out of it. Helping someone and seeing what a difference it makes in their life will be a source of encouragement and joy to you.

HEALTH CHECKLIST

- 😊 **When was the last time I helped someone without expecting anything in return?**

- 😊 **Do I truly put into practice the command to "Do to others as you would have them do to you" (Luke 6: 31) at all times?**

- 😊 **Have I ever thought about doing some voluntary work in my community?**

> *"...if you spend yourselves on behalf of the hungry and satisfy the needs of the oppressed, then your light will rise in the darkness, and your night will become like the noonday."*
> *Isaiah 58: 10*

9. CULTIVATE WORSHIP AS A LIFESTYLE

The word "worship" is often used to refer to communal singing and, more specifically, the part of such a time when quieter songs are sung. However, worship is about much more than singing songs—it should be a way of life for all Christians.

True worship pleases God because it reveals the attitude of your heart. He is looking for worshippers, not simply worship. He hates it when Christians simply attend church on a Sunday, sing a few songs without meaning what they sing, and think they have worshipped Him. This is what God says about such worship: "These people come near to me with their mouth and honor me with their lips, but their hearts are far from me. Their worship of me is made up only of rules taught by men." (*Isaiah 29: 13*).

MADE FOR WORSHIP

Worship is natural, as natural as breathing. You are wired for worship; if you aren't

RIGHT **Worship is not just about going to church—God wants your love at all times.**

God wants to ignite a spark of passion in you and captivate your heart. Your spiritual life is all about your relationship with Him. He longs for your love, which will only ever be a tiny percentage of the immeasurable love He gives back to you. Regularly take a time out to reflect on who God is, and the amazing things He has done. Your worship stems from your knowledge of who He is. Proclaim what the Bible says about God's character: He is just, holy, mighty, a tender father, compassionate, and slow to anger.

There may be times when the feeling doesn't flow naturally out of your heart and you actively have to choose to worship and love God. Don't be discouraged—this is the same as in any romantic relationship. When you first discover your true love you are completely bowled over. You can't get enough of the person, but as the years go by this initial feeling may die down and you may need to work harder at keeping the love alive. It doesn't mean you love the person any less, and you will probably experience far greater depths to your love over time, but it is important to recognize how familiarity changes a relationship.

ABOVE **True worship involves giving over your whole life to God, completely surrendering to Him.**

worshipping God then you will find a substitute—whether it is yourself, someone else, or an inanimate object. However, everything else will leave you with a feeling of emptiness. God is the source of all life so you won't feel satisfied worshipping anything else. This should motivate your desire to stay close to Him and learn that real worship is about submitting the whole of yourself to Him.

There may be times when it feels as though circumstances are conspiring against you, but God may allow this to happen in order to teach you to be totally dependent on Him. God is to be your source and sustainer—nothing else should be in His place.

TAKING YOUR SPIRITUAL PULSE

WORSHIP AT ALL TIMES

"Whatever you do, work at it with all your heart, as working for the Lord, not for men." (*Colossians 3: 24*). You should worship God in everything you do—whether it is making breakfast, working at a busy job, or putting your kids to bed. If you relegate your worship purely

to church meetings then you're in danger of becoming spiritually sick, because you are shutting off the majority of your life from the God who sustains it all. Wherever you are, whatever you're doing, imagine that you're doing it before God as an act of worship. Invite Him into every part of your life. He longs to be with you at all times, but isn't pushy. He'll remain in the background unless you ask Him to join you.

ABOVE AND RIGHT **In the middle of your busy life you can still tell God how much you love Him.**

HEALTH CHECKLIST

- Do I view worship as simply singing songs?

- Are there any things in my life that I "worship"?

- Is my lifestyle an act of worship?

- In what areas of my life could I improve this?

COMMUNAL WORSHIP TIMES

When you have learned to cultivate a worshipful heart, coming together for a communal period of church worship becomes an even more powerful experience. You don't need to spend time getting into His presence—you will have been abiding there all week anyway.

Speaking of His mighty deeds, praising Him together, and allowing His Spirit to move you through the use of spiritual gifts (see page 91) will give glory back to Him while also igniting faith in you. Meeting together like this reminds you that worship is all about God, and through it your spirit will be encouraged to stand firm.

"...offer your bodies as living sacrifices, holy and pleasing to God—this is your spiritual act of worship." Romans 12: 1

TOP TIP

As soon as you wake up tomorrow, tell God how much you love Him.

TAKING YOUR SPIRITUAL PULSE

10. BE ACCOUNTABLE

A *thletes often train with a partner. The other person helps to keep them motivated and can also point out where the athlete's technique could be improved. Having the same sort of relationship with another Christian will help you in your spiritual life, as well as provide support. They can offer insights from a different point of view that you might have missed by yourself.*

Most people hate letting others see that they are less than perfect, and yet, this is an important way to grow as a Christian. Admitting that you're finding the Christian life difficult and being humble enough to allow someone else to point out the sin in your life are signs of maturity. To achieve this, find yourself an accountability partner who is prepared to be totally honest with you—one who will challenge you when necessary. Your accountability partner will need to

TO
T

This week wri
short list of people
think you could
accountable to. Ask God v
the right person is, t
go and speak to t
person abou

> *"Two are better than one, because they have a good return for their work: If one falls down, his friend can help him up."*
>
> *Ecclesiastes 4: 9–10*

be a close friend who you know will act out of love at all times. You will have to allow yourself to be vulnerable in front of this person, so don't choose someone who will be too harshly judgmental. Remember that it is a partnership, so you must be prepared to do the same for them and they should be open to that.

Before you start being accountable, check that you're both totally happy with the arrangement and pray that God will always help you to encourage each other. Every time you meet, ask each other how disciplined you're being in your devotional times, how your closest relationships are, and how you are dealing with particular moral or behavioral struggles. Basically, everything to do with your relationship with God and other people. You will find that being accountable will spur you on to keep a check on your thoughts and actions. Even if your initial motivation is not

wanting your friend to discover you've blown it again, you will be cultivating a useful discipline.

ASKING FOR HELP

As you worked through the checkup in the previous chapter, you may have found that particular areas were especially difficult for you. These would be good topics to discuss with your accountability partner, because he or she will be able to support and encourage you while you seek to change.

When you're finding it difficult to cope with temptation, admitting it to someone you trust is often the first positive step in overcoming it. So do not be afraid to open up and admit some of the struggles you're having. By doing this, you will help your partner to do the same.

LEFT **Just as an athlete has a helper, find a partner who will help you "train" and keep disciplined.**

HEALTH CHECKLIST

☺ *Does finding an "accountability partner" terrify me? Why is that?*

☺ *Could I be totally honest with someone else about everything I struggle with?*

Dealing with problems and difficulties

The cares of this world can throttle your spiritual life; some invade slowly but surely like a cancer, while others strike suddenly like a heart attack. But there are spiritual prescriptions that can help you deal with the problems you will undoubtedly encounter. Whether big or small, these problems all deserve attention because, if left unchecked, they could have a serious impact on your spiritual life.

TAKING YOUR SPIRITUAL PULSE

WHEN THE BIBLE SEEMS STALE

The Bible is the inspired word of God so what can you do if you find reading it has become a duty rather than a pleasure? Be honest with yourself. Rather than reaching for your Bible with happy anticipation, do you grit your teeth and just get on with reading a little bit each day because you think you ought to? If so, how can you revive the experience to make it fresh and invigorating again?

Remind yourself that discipline is an important aspect of faith. Western culture conditions us to expect instant results, but long-term benefits to your spirit require persistence as well as belief. It isn't enough simply to sit back and allow others to spoonfeed you passages from the Bible once a week rather than delving into it for yourself.

Reflect on what the Bible is— God's word for Christians. You should feel privileged that you are able to read it each day. Because you cannot know God deeply without knowing His word, try asking Him to breathe life into what you read. Read actively rather than always returning to familiar and reassuring passages. There are plenty of challenges to be found in the Bible if you set out to look for them.

LEFT **It takes time to gain the most benefit from reading the Bible. Try to set aside a portion of each day to read it.**

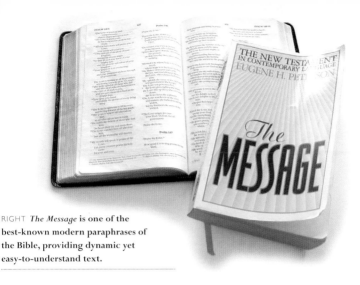

RIGHT *The Message* is one of the
best-known modern paraphrases of
the Bible, providing dynamic yet
easy-to-understand text.

TRYING SOMETHING NEW

Have you always spent the same
amount of time each day reading
the Bible, using the same set of
teaching notes? Set routines can
take away some of the freshness
and excitement the Bible offers.
Try a different approach! If you
usually read a long passage
without stopping, try looking at
just a few verses, then spend
time meditating on them, asking
yourself what they mean and
how you can apply them to your
own life. You could also try
memorizing a few verses.

If you use a set of teaching
notes or helpful Bible tools, try
varying them on a regular basis.
There is an enormous variety
of Bible reference books
available that you might consider
purchasing. You can also try
reading the Bible in different
translations and compare the
texts. Or why not choose a
particular book of the Bible or a
character to focus on? You could
also pick a theme and use a
concordance to find relevant
verses that will take you on an
adventure through the whole
Bible. These suggestions should
inspire you to think more
creatively and to see the Bible
in a fresh way.

*"How can a young man keep his
way pure? By living according to
your word...I have hidden your
word in my heart that I might
not sin against you."*
Psalm 119: 9 and 11

REMEDY TIP

☺ *Ask God to inspire you
as you actively read.*

WHEN PRAYER SEEMS UNINSPIRED

Praying allows direct communication with the creator of the universe, so why do so many Christians find it immensely difficult to pray?

If you are being honest, would you say that you find it a real struggle to motivate yourself to pray each day? Don't feel disheartened. You're not alone and there are some simple steps that you can take to turn your prayer life into a more dynamic experience.

Being a Christian involves discipline. There will be days when you don't feel like reading the Bible, praying, and serving others, but it's still important to continue doing these things. Athletes don't stop training because it's becoming a hard ordeal—they keep their end goal in sight at all times. You should do the same with any spiritual discipline you are finding difficult.

God wants you to pray, but, thankfully, there is more to it than that! God doesn't just want you to cultivate the discipline of prayer without truly engaging in it—He is desperate to talk to you. So take the time to listen quietly as well as talk.

ABOVE LEFT **God is the creator of the whole universe and yet He wants to spend time with you!**

BELOW **Sometimes prayer can seem very difficult but try to persevere during these times.**

THE LORD'S PRAYER

If you find it difficult to pray, then you should look to the example that Jesus provided. The Lord's Prayer starts by recognizing and honoring God, and indicates the close relationship Christians can have with Him. Then it encourages active submission to God, and indicates our desire that His rule and will be carried out all over the world. Only after you have put God first in this way can you ask Him for anything.

Jesus indicates what He thinks is most important—not material gain but spiritual nourishment, forgiveness, and deliverance from evil. Your spiritual being needs these elements to stay healthy.

"This, then is how you should pray:

> *Our Father in heaven,*
> *hallowed be your name,*
> *your kingdom come,*
> *your will be done*
> *on earth as it is in heaven.*
> *Give us today our daily*
> *bread.*
> *Forgive us our debts,*
> *as we also have forgiven our*
> *debtors.*
> *And lead us not into*
> *temptation, but deliver us*
> *from the evil one. "*
> *Matthew 6: 9–13*

This prayer is helpful because it keeps your focus intact. Use the same kind of approach when you pray your own prayers. Start by spending time focusing on who God is before presenting your requests. You will probably find that as you praise God He takes up greater residence in your mind, and your problems will seem much smaller as a result.

TRY VARIATION

It's important to spend time alone with God each day, but also try praying with friends so you can spur one another on. Praying with a spouse or your family is beneficial, too, because it strengthens your bond. Try using portions of scripture as meditations that lead you into prayer, or work through a book of prayer written by someone else.

ABOVE **Sharing and praying with a close friend can encourage you, especially if you are finding life difficult.**

WHEN DOUBTS CREEP IN

Every Christian experiences worrisome doubts at some point in their life. You need to be confident in the reason for your faith in order to communicate it effectively to nonbelievers. There is nothing wrong with thinking about, or even questioning, aspects of your faith.

ABOVE **Do you find that there are times when you wonder about your faith? You are not alone.**

Without doubts, your faith couldn't grow; doubts are like weights that your faith must lift in order to become strong. However, if your doubts keep returning and you stumble under the weight of them, this can be a huge hindrance to your spiritual life. Be aware that the devil wants to stop you from growing as a Christian. When you doubt, ask yourself if you are genuinely seeking after the truth. Doubt in itself is not wrong but it can turn into unbelief when you start to let it take hold of you.

It's possible to stop the seeds of doubt from becoming unbelief. Christians profess that they believe God has saved them, and the Holy Spirit testifies to this directly (*Romans 8: 16*).

However, Christians may at times question whether God truly loves them or whether they really are children of God. Do these questions sound familiar? Sometimes they are the result of disobeying God—you feel defeated by sin and this allows doubts to creep in and can leave you vulnerable to temptation. If you pinpoint the sin and confess it, peace should replace doubt.

Intellectual doubts often stem from an incorrect view of God. It can be easy to believe what your culture teaches about Him, rather than looking to the Bible for the whole truth (*see opposite*).

It's important to use the tools that God gave you to help overcome doubts (see *Ephesians 6: 13–18*). He knows that the devil will seek to confuse you, so He has given you the Bible to help you to combat any lies that are fed to you. The Bible is full of truths about your salvation and your identity in Christ as a child of God who is capable of overcoming adversity. You can also ask God to help you by revealing Himself to you in new ways, particularly in the areas where you're struggling.

Don't forget that He has provided you with Christian friends. And don't be afraid to chat about your doubts with mature Christians as well as those who have overcome similar doubts (see Be Accountable, *page 54*). It is when you openly admit your doubts that you can begin to deal with them honestly.

As you mature as a Christian, you will learn to trust God and actively choose to believe rather than doubt. James says that those who constantly doubt are like waves of the sea, always being blown about

(*James 1: 6*). That is why it's important to be part of a church that provides solid biblical teaching. The church will help you grow in your knowledge of God's word and become more stable in your spiritual life (see Attend Church, *pages 30–31*).

Ultimately, Christianity is a journey that requires faith. Don't expect to get all the answers this side of heaven. Remember, God will provide all you need to keep spiritually fit but He also wants you to take steps of faith.

REMEDY TIP

😊 *Let God's word help you overcome doubts.*

RIGHT **Learning to trust God, even in the midst of doubts, will help you to build up spiritual muscle.**

TAKING YOUR SPIRITUAL PULSE

WHEN ANGER OVERWHELMS YOU

*D*o *you find that anger flares up almost out of nowhere and you become a totally different person—one that you are ashamed of? Or do you try to suppress your anger until you feel as though you are about to explode, then all of a sudden it bursts out and everything gets messy? Why is it that anger can have such a hold on human beings?*

It's important to recognize that anger is not wrong in itself. After all Jesus was angry with the people who used the temple as a marketplace. Too often Christians are taught that anger is a negative emotion and therefore they think they should suppress it rather than admit their feelings. Unfortunately this won't solve anything.

It's important to be honest about the way you feel while also looking at at how you react to that feeling. It is at the point when you lose control that you fall into sin. As *Proverbs 14: 17* says: "A quick-tempered man does foolish things." But be reassured, all behavior patterns are learned so this lack of control can be "unlearned" and changed.

REACTING IN THE RIGHT WAY

So how can you behave in a godly way when you start to feel angry? The most important thing to do is to step back from the situation that caused the anger.

Next, try and work out why you're feeling angry. Anger is a symptom of something, not the root cause; it could be due to a hurt, fear, or frustration. It may be a "righteous anger"—you feel frustrated at an injustice you are seeing—in which case there is nothing wrong with standing up for the truth.

When looking for the cause of your anger, pray and ask God to help you be honest. You may feel hurt and angry at the way someone has treated you and yet, when you look more closely, you find that it reveals more about you than the person you are angry with. If it brings up personal issues, you need to readdress your attention toward yourself and work through them. The anger could be due to someone hitting a raw nerve, which stems from one of your insecurities.

Anger is often due to past hurts, so if you experience

ABOVE **Sometimes it can be helpful to sit down and work through past hurts with someone else.**

recurring anger examine the triggers. Are there particular patterns? If you pinpoint a past hurt, you will need to work through it and reach a point of forgiveness to free yourself (*see* Learn to Forgive, *pages 44–47*).

If you get to a place where you truly believe that someone has treated you unfairly and it's necessary to confront him or her, remember that anger should always be tempered with compassion. Of course you should speak the truth, but it should always be done with love. You will need to forgive them, no matter how they respond to you. In some cases, it's a good idea to seek out a more mature Christian to discuss the situation with you before taking any action.

LEFT **Don't allow your anger to explode, because you will just regret it later.**

REMEDY TIP

☺ *Try to work out why you are angry.*

TAKING YOUR SPIRITUAL PULSE

WHEN FEAR AND WORRY TAKE HOLD

*F*ears and anxieties grip many people, including Christians. To a certain extent this is understandable, given the unstable state of the world these days. However, as someone who believes and trusts in God, you do not need to allow fear and worry to paralyze your spiritual life.

BELOW **God is your Father—He longs to take hold of your hand and guide you through life.**

Do you have an overwhelming sense of fear that pervades almost every area of your life? Fear often results from lack of trust, but who better to trust than God? It's important to remember that He is your father and He loves and accepts you exactly as you are.

Doesn't it say in the Bible that "perfect love drives out fear?" Meditate on the fact that God's love is perfect and unconditional. It may be that you are trying to trust Him but you're unable to let go of the reins of your life completely—perhaps because you aren't entirely convinced of the direction in which He's taking you. However, God only allows whatever is for your good, so relax and believe that He's looking after your best interests. Even if He allows you to go through a difficult time, it's

RIGHT **Take time to relax and meditate on God's perfect love.**

because He is working out His purposes in you. As a father He will discipline you and will want to see you grow spiritually but His discipline is always done out of love (see When Tragedy Hits, pages 76–77).

THE WORRIES OF LIFE

Sometimes it can be easier to tackle the bigger fears and let the everyday stresses of modern living remain unchecked. How do you cope with these? Remember that God is interested in all the little details of your life—He may be all-seeing and all-knowing, but He still wants you to include Him in every part of your life. And He knows that worry can be a common problem for Christians. That's why Jesus taught on it while He walked the earth: "…do not worry about what you will eat or drink; or about your body, what you will wear. Is not life more important than food, and the body more important

than clothes? … Who of you by worrying can add a single hour to his life?" (*Matthew 6: 25, 27*). Jesus is teaching about a change of perspective.

Do you find that you're anxious because you focus on your problems? Take your eyes off your problems for a moment and look heavenward. God is in charge of everything—He cares for you. A simple perspective change can wipe away stressful worries (see When Prayer Seems Uninspired, *pages 60–61*). Ask God to help you, as the Bible says: "Do not be anxious about anything, but in everything, by prayer and petition, with thanksgiving, present your requests to God." (*Philippians 4: 6*).

REMEDY TIP

😊 **Work at truly believing that God is in control.**

67

WHEN GUILT LINGERS

Nothing stifles spiritual life like guilt. God loves, accepts, and forgives His people and yet Christians are often wracked with guilt. They can't see beyond it. Are you such a person? Even after you've said sorry to God for a particular sin, do you still feel guilty for that action even hours, or perhaps days later?

It is important to recognize that God uses guilt as a trigger. In this instance it is the Holy Spirit nudging at your conscience. He is like the nerve ending that tells a finger touching fire that it is likely to get burned! Guilt can be a warning that you have unconfessed sin in your life that is a danger to your spiritual well-being. If guilt is lingering, start by honestly assessing yourself to ensure there is no underlying sin.

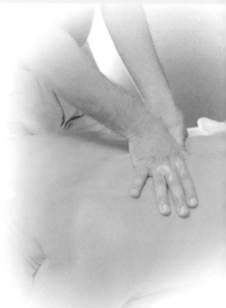

ABOVE **The Holy Spirit will gently put His finger on problem areas, such as unconfessed sin.**

If you're still feeling guilty, it is probably because you haven't forgiven yourself for the sin. You may believe that God truly forgives you when you confess your sin, but somehow you can't forgive yourself. The reasons behind this normally stem from guilt, which often leads to fear and even pride. You may not be able to get past the feeling that somehow you deserve to be punished. The devil will keep reminding you of how awful you have been. If this is your experience, you simply *have* to accept that Jesus took all your punishment for every sin you will ever commit when He died on the cross. By dwelling on feelings of guilt you are actually belittling what He did.

God's way is to bring your sin to the forefront so as to give you an opportunity to confess it (*see* Confess Your Sins, *pages 38–39*). Once you have done so, as far as God is concerned, it is forgotten and He wants you to move on. So by not forgiving yourself and letting go of the feelings of guilt you are dishonoring God. Consciously make a decision to let go each time you confess something (*see* Learn to Forgive, *pages 44–47*).

FALSE GUILT

The other possibility may be that you are experiencing false guilt. This is when you feel guilty even though you haven't done anything wrong. It is often the result of an overactive conscience that is driven by the unfair expectations of others, or even your own unreasonably high standards. Perhaps you

don't feel good enough. In the back of your mind everything you do falls short of some rule you've built up in your mind. Again, it is a case of learning to let go. God didn't set all these unfair expectations, and He knows that you aren't going to be perfect this side of heaven. Still, He accepts you as you are.

Remind yourself that your salvation is due to grace, and not to your own works of goodness. Don't allow false guilt to prevent you from making progress in your spiritual journey.

REMEDY TIP

☺ *Learn to let go and truly forgive yourself.*

BELOW **Let go of false guilt and feel the weight drop away from you.**

TAKING YOUR SPIRITUAL PULSE

WHEN YOU FEEL LIKE A FAILURE

*W*hen you've worked really hard at being spiritually disciplined, it can be disheartening when you suddenly stumble and make a mistake. What should you do when you feel as though you've blown it? How can you pick yourself up and carry on without looking back?

The most important thing is to realize that God loves you no matter what you do—you cannot make Him love you more or less. He has accepted you as His son or daughter and He knows that you will sometimes stumble. He isn't standing over you, waiting to tell you off. He is ready to pick you up, dust you off, and send you on your way again.

LEFT **Even in the middle of your shame and feelings of failure, God is looking at you lovingly, wanting to help you.**

LEARNING FROM YOUR FAILURES

Although everyone hates failure, it's an inevitable part of being human—no one is perfect. Athletes don't give up if they don't win their first race; they realize their career is developing and they use each experience to motivate them to work harder. This is also the way you should view your failures. The trick is to learn from them. That is what God wants you to do. Making a mistake doesn't make you a bad person. You can mature significantly through failing!

If you dwell on your failure and allow it to take you in a downward spiral then you've missed the point. Successful people see beyond their failures, and learn how to use them. You may cringe at your own life

ABOVE **Realize that failure can teach you important lessons—and learning from failure is often the first step on the road to success.**

and the things you fail at over and over again, but the Bible is full of people who failed and God still used them greatly— so take heart.

What about David? He committed adultery and murder and yet God called Him a man after His own heart! Your failings do not disqualify you from being used by God, but your reaction to them could. Don't let yourself get tied up in knots. This simply means you are preventing yourself from being effective in your spiritual life.

Next time you fail at something, meet the failure head on. If you've sinned, ask for forgiveness but then let go. Don't allow yourself to feel condemned, because God has already mercifully forgotten what you did. Sometimes, however, failure isn't about doing

> *"Therefore, there is no condemnation for those who are in Christ Jesus."*
> *Romans 8: 1*

something wrong. Perhaps a situation hasn't worked out exactly as you thought it would. You feel like a failure while, in fact, God is working things out to His purposes. At all times look at what God could be teaching you through the experience. Learning to deal with failure effectively is a sign of maturity and that is the aim of your spiritual life after all.

REMEDY TIP

☺ *Learn to let your failures motivate you.*

71

WHEN GOD SEEMS FAR AWAY

Have you ever gone through periods when you feel as though God has deserted you? When you pray does it sometimes feel as though you are talking to a brick wall rather than to your heavenly Father? Why do Christians have these times when God feels distant, and what can you do when you find yourself seemingly cut off from the source of all life?

Rather than immediately getting angry and struggling to find out why God has deserted you, realize that Christians can unconsciously take a step back from God by sinning. Therefore, if He feels distant, you should use that as a prompt to question whether you have allowed sin to creep in unchecked.

If you're sure that you haven't disobeyed God, it can be bewildering if He still feels far away. However, God sometimes takes a step back and allows people to go through wilderness experiences to test how much they want fellowship with Him, and how much they depend on and trust Him. This is exactly what He did to Hezekiah: "God left him to test him and to know everything that was in his heart." (*2 Chronicles 32: 31*). It is through such struggles that maturity develops and, although it may

> *"How long, O Lord? Will you forget me for ever? How long will you hide your face from me? How long must I wrestle with my thoughts and every day have sorrow in my heart?"*
> *Psalm 13: 1–2*

not feel like it, God *is* standing close by you at all times.

There are countless examples in the Bible of God using wilderness experiences to teach His people. Abraham is one. God promised him that he would be the father of nations and yet he had to wait years and years, until he and Sarah were way past the age when they could naturally conceive. It must have felt as though God had completely deserted them, but in Hebrews they are noted for their faith. Of course God kept His promise in the end!

Often the silence that Christians have is simply God pausing, waiting for them to cultivate faith. Receiving specific, detailed guidance for every step of your life doesn't encourage spiritual development but seeking God and acting in faith does.

LEFT **Every Christian goes through desert experiences in their life—often God allows it to help you cultivate faith.**

TELLING GOD
HOW YOU FEEL

It's okay to express how you feel during such an experience. The Psalms are full of writers telling God when they are struggling (see *left*). God can cope with whatever emotions you are going through so pour them out to Him. If you are unsure how to start, look at the Psalms and use them as a basis for your own prayers. As you read through them, take comfort from the fact that you aren't the only person who has ever felt this way.

You should also reflect on truths about who God is. These will feed your spirit. Even when the psalmists were struggling, they spoke directly to their souls: "Why are you downcast, O my soul? Why so disturbed within me? Put your hope in God, for I will yet praise him, my Savior and my God." (*Psalm 42: 5–6*). After you come out the other side, you will be able to look back and see how the experience has changed you for the better. That was God's purpose from the outset.

REMEDY TIP

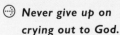 **Never give up on crying out to God.**

WHEN IMPATIENCE IS YOUR CONSTANT COMPANION

We live in a society where instant results are expected. This trend will probably have had an effect on you, both in your physical and spiritual life. Do you, for example, find that you are often impatient with those around you and even with God Himself? What is it that drives this feeling and what can you do about it?

ABOVE **Are you constantly rushing around, trying to beat the clock? This lifestyle could make you impatient.**

If you're honest, do you wish sometimes that God would hurry up and answer your prayers in the way that you want Him to? Most Christians at some point in their spiritual journey want God to take action when it suits them, rather waiting for his timing! However, it's important to realize that being impatient with God shows a lack of trust, faith, and submission to Him.

Remember, His ways are higher than yours and so you need to surrender in humility to His authority. After all, He is God. You might think something is exactly what you need at a given moment, but God knows better than you. He will often make you wait for things to test and refine your faith, to exercise and build your patience, and to teach you the need to persevere in prayer.

WHEN YOU ARE IMPATIENT WITH OTHERS

You might become impatient with other people when they aren't carrying out tasks in the way you would or aren't doing them as quickly or as well as you think you could. Here your impatience is really an issue of pride, which is a sinful attitude.

How would you like it if someone told you that you weren't doing something the right way? Take a step back from such situations to see it from both sides. Why is your way right and the other person's wrong? Even if they aren't doing something as well as you would, you should view it as an opportunity for them. By responding with impatience, you could suffocate their growth. They could end up being too frightened to try something new next time they are asked. Especially within a church, where the emphasis is on family, such intolerance could break down the unity in relationships.

God tells you to love and accept everyone and to show the respect that you want to be shown, even if you don't agree with the way they do things! (*See* Attend Church, *pages 30–31*.)

Every person is equal in God's eyes, so seeing yourself as better than someone else is a distorted view. As has been said before, God will judge you with the measure that you use to judge others. So learn to keep a close check on your responses to other people. He may be using them to point out to you that you need to deal with your impatience.

RIGHT **Be patient and encouraging when others are learning something new.**

REMEDY TIP

😊 *Learn to trust that God's way is best.*

WHEN TRAGEDY HITS

Perhaps you've just heard that you've lost your job, you've recently been diagnosed with a long-term illness, or a loved one has passed away. How do you deal with such unexpected suffering without it snuffing out your faith? And what about suffering in general? As a Christian, are you supposed to be free of it or is it an inevitable part of life?

LEFT **If you are in despair or suffering, open up to God and tell Him how you are feeling.**

It's important to remind yourself at this time that God is a loving, just God. The experiences you're going through may not seem fair but that does not mean that God has changed who He is. You can still trust Him to act in your best interests. Open up to Him and be honest about how you are feeling. Remember that God can empathize with you—after all He watched His beloved son die. He knows your distress, the depths of your pain, and is there to comfort you. He is suffering with you and through this you can experience a closer communion with Him, which couldn't be achieved in any other way.

WHY DO CHRISTIANS SUFFER?

While God doesn't purposefully afflict you, He sometimes allows difficult things to happen because they will help to make you more like Jesus. Too often Christians cry out to God to deliver them from suffering without looking to see what they might learn from the situation. This may seem like a hard thing to do, particularly if you are facing deep tragedy, but remember how much Jesus suffered for you. The road of a disciple isn't an easy one but you have a deep-rooted hope and can look forward to eternal life with your Maker. Rather than dwelling on the "why" issue, which will just take you in a downward spiral and drive a wedge between you and God, try asking God what He specifically wants to teach you through this experience.

> *"We also rejoice in our sufferings, because we know that suffering produces perseverance; perseverance character; and character, hope."* Romans 5: 3–4

As a human, you are part of a fallen world in which bad things happen to everyone. If God protected you from any form of suffering, you wouldn't be able to relate to those around you. You are the vehicle through which God has chosen to reveal His love. You can connect with others through suffering and tragedy. While you may not be able to control what happens to you, you can control the way in which you respond when suffering occurs.

Remember that your spiritual life is a journey in which you will face many trials and difficulties. God uses suffering to prepare you for entering heaven with increased glory. As Paul said: "Therefore we do not lose heart. Though outwardly we are wasting away, yet inwardly we are being renewed day by day. For our light and momentary troubles are achieving for us an eternal glory that far outweighs them all." (*2 Corinthians 4: 16–17*).

REMEDY TIP

😊 **Ask God what this experience can teach you.**

BELOW **As a Christian you have the hope of a bright future.**

Keeping in shape

You have pinpointed the areas that you need to work at more diligently and picked up some tips on how to improve your spiritual life, but how do you maintain it once it is in a healthy state? What follows is some advice on how to keep your life in balance. Remember that keeping in shape, whether you are working on your body or spirit, requires discipline. You need to keep cultivating discipline to prevent your spiritual body from becoming flabby!

BALANCING YOUR DIET

There is a huge emphasis on eating a healthy diet these days. Although most people are incredibly busy, they take the time to ensure they are feeding their bodies the right kinds of food. You should take the time to ensure that your spiritual diet is as well balanced as your nutritional one.

ABOVE **Avoid junk food for the soul; your spiritual life can only develop properly if it's fed a good diet.**

SPIRITUAL WELL-BEING

It is obvious that humans can't survive without a balanced diet, so why is it that so many Christians tend to ignore their spiritual well-being? The same principles that ensure a healthy body—taking in a good range of healthy nutrients and eating everything in moderation rather than overdoing it on favorite foods—can be applied to your spiritual diet, too.

Every Christian is well aware of the importance of spending time in prayer and with other Christians, just as almost everyone is aware of the different components that make up a nutritionally sound diet. However, putting that knowledge into practice is much harder, especially if you find your life is becoming over-full. The "Sources of Nourishment" pyramid (*opposite*) may give you some food for thought.

HEALTH CHECKLIST

☺ *Was my time too full today for me to even think about my faith?*

☺ *Have I listened to God as well as prayed to Him in the last few days?*

☺ *How much time have I spent with other Christians this week?*

SOURCES OF NOURISHMENT

PRAYER
Communicate with God on a regular basis, because He wants to be a part of your whole life.

WORSHIP
Spend time alone in God's presence, as well as with other people.

SHARING YOUR FAITH
Be ready to explain what you believe in and why.

FELLOWSHIP
Spend quality time with other Christians as often as possible.

DISCIPLESHIP
A close, honest relationship with a mature Christian can teach you a lot.

BIBLE STUDY
Read and meditate on a portion of scripture each day.

PRAYER

Remember that prayer is simply talking with God. He's interested in all parts of your life so try speaking to Him throughout the day.

SHARING YOUR FAITH

You grow spiritually by giving as well as receiving and God has called you to speak to others rather than keeping the good news to yourself.

BIBLE STUDY

Ensure that you read the Bible every day. It's often helpful to make time for this first thing in the morning.

WORSHIP

God deserves your praise and worship so it's important to spend time in His presence, both alone and with other people. Worship is about more than just singing songs—it is a lifestyle that reflects what you believe.

FELLOWSHIP

When you spend time with other Christians, you build up your faith. Group discussions can provide you with different, helpful perspectives on scripture.

DISCIPLESHIP

One of the best ways to grow is to learn from more mature Christians. They will be able to encourage you and challenge you in your faith. You can do the same for "younger" Christians.

FIT TIP

Use this week to balance your spiritual diet. Look at the nourishment pyramid and pinpoint the "nutrients" you aren't giving yourself. Work at adding them into your diet.

YOU ARE WHAT YOU EAT

Whatever you put into your mind will emerge in your words and actions, so be careful what you feed it. Do you have a problem with impure daydreams or thoughts? If so, be careful of the television programs and movies you watch, the books and magazines you read, and the conversations you take part in.

Are you ever embarrassed, even shocked, by what comes out of your mouth? The tongue, as James says in scripture, is a small part of your body and yet it can be deadly. It is fed by what you take in, and it also reflects your inner nature. As Jesus said: "The things that come out of the mouth come from the heart, and these make a man 'unclean.' For out of the heart come evil thoughts, murder, adultery, sexual immorality, theft, false testimony, slander." (*Matthew 15: 18–19*).

AVOIDING "JUNK FOOD"

You now know the elements that make up a balanced spiritual diet, but there is also a lot of garbage out there that Christians passively allow themselves to absorb. The media bombards you with images and ideas wherever you turn, and a lot of them are not helpful or uplifting for your spiritual being. It is your responsibility to switch off or change channels whenever you come across something you know you shouldn't be looking at. This same principle is true when dealing with temptation— turn away from it to avoid the aggravation!

ABOVE **Do you find gossip enticing? Be careful, since this will affect who you are.**

It is easy to get caught up in unhealthy conversations at work and at home. These conversations seem to start innocently enough, but then turn to talking about someone behind their back, or lustfully discussing a character seen on television the night before. Although you may not actively join in, just being there could have an effect on you because your mind is absorbing what you are hearing. At all times you should be thinking, "What would I do if Jesus was standing next to me?"—because He is! It's simple enough to make your excuses and leave the group if necessary.

LEARNING TO REPLACE THOUGHTS

If you struggle with particular thoughts, counter them by looking up what God says about them. Learn relevant scriptures by heart so when an unhealthy thought pops into your mind you can overrule it. This is what is meant by the phrase: "…be transformed by the renewing of your mind." (*Romans 12: 2*).

If you struggle with impure thoughts, for example, and

"Whatever is true, whatever is noble, whatever is right, whatever is pure, whatever is lovely, whatever is admirable— if anything is excellent or praiseworthy—think about such things." *Philippians 4: 8*

recognize that they could lead to impure actions, reflect on the following: "Flee from sexual immorality… do you not know that your body is a temple of the Holy Spirit?" (*1 Corinthians 6: 18–19*). If you feel that resisting such thoughts is too difficult, consider that the Bible tells you that you can "…take captive every thought to make it obedient to Christ." (*2 Corinthians 10: 5*). Start practicing this discipline today.

FIT TIP

Meditate on a short Psalm each morning this week.

RIGHT **Spend time "feeding" on the words contained within the Bible.**

BALANCING YOUR FRIENDSHIPS

*W*hat with church, small groups, and close Christian friends you might find you have little time left to build relationships with work colleagues, neighbors, and the people you come across each day. So how can you balance your friendships effectively?

BELOW **Christians and nonbelievers can share common interests and enjoy spending time together.**

Christians sometimes segregate themselves from other people. It's as if they're scared they might get tarnished if they engage with anyone who isn't a Christian. However, Jesus calls His people to be salt and light in the world. You are one of His representatives on earth so hiding away with Christians for the rest of your life is not the answer.

> *"You are the light of the world...let your light shine before men, that they may see your good deeds and praise your Father in heaven."*
> Matthew 5: 14 and 16

It's true that if you spend all your time with people who could influence you negatively you are setting yourself up for difficulties (see page 83). You

ABOVE **If you don't mix with nonbelievers much, think about joining a local club.**

FIT TIP

Think of someone who doesn't know you are a Christian. Pray today for the opportunity to tell them.

need to make sure that you have strong, supportive Christian friendships that will not only encourage you in your faith but will also help you reach out to those around you who may not share your beliefs. Jesus was friends with all sorts of people—not just those who were similar to Him or who agreed with Him all the time!

FRIENDSHIP EVANGELISM

People who are frightened of "witnessing" often think of a Christian who appears completely fearless, such as one who stands on a street corner and shouts out what it means to be saved. Don't worry—that is not the only way to share

your faith. So if you cringe at the thought of doing that, and think that your friends would, too, you shouldn't feel condemned!

There are other ways to show God's love to the world. One of the best ways to do that is through what is known as friendship evangelism. This involves cultivating friendships, not out of a desire to chalk up another conversion (it isn't for you anyway) but just in order to love them. There are countless stories of people recognizing that God has touched them through acts of kindness carried out by Christians who have appeared alongside them and simply been their friend.

TAKING YOUR SPIRITUAL PULSE

BALANCING YOUR TIME

D*o you long to put all the spiritual disciplines that you've read about in this book into practice in your life, but can't see how you will manage because you're just too busy? Do you rush from one activity to another, without time to draw breath? How can you ensure you have time for your spiritual life?*

ABOVE **Rather than constantly running from one chore to another, take time out to reflect on what is most important.**

If your life is crowded by people and problems vying for your time, try putting God first. Give Him the first few moments when you wake up before all the pressures crowd into your brain. Then you might find that the rest of your day is more productive. This is a similar principle to tithing. He wants you to give Him your best—and that includes your time—so "…seek first his kingdom and his righteousness, and all these things will be given to you as well." (*Matthew 6: 33*).

There is a saying that you can be "too busy not to pray." What this means is that it is at the very times when you are most stressed that you need to be sure you take time out to spend

with God. When you do this, try asking Him to help you prioritize your time. He is interested in the little details and that includes setting daily goals and workloads (see When Fear and Worry Take Hold, *pages 66–67*) .

If you truly understand that there are specific roles God wants you to fulfill at home, at work, and in church, you can look to Him to direct you before making decisions about what you will do. It may be that He will ask you to take a break from an activity—perhaps to allow you to concentrate on something else. Maybe He wants to re-energize you, or maybe He wants to give someone else the opportunity to move into that role for a season. If the thought of giving something up feels difficult, just remember that you won't be an effective Christian if you are totally stressed or burned out. You need to be able to say no sometimes.

"Even youths grow tired and weary, and young men stumble and fall; but those who hope in the Lord will renew their strength." Isaiah 40: 30–31

GIVING YOURSELF SPACE

With all the talk of serving others and putting them before yourself, you could be forgiven for thinking that there isn't any time left for you! But of course you need to receive from God in order to be able to give out effectively. Just as all forms of exercise incorporate a winding-down period at the end of the session. You need to build in time when you can draw close to God, worship and rest in His presence, and allow Him to refresh you.

It's also important to take time out to rest your physical body as well as your spiritual

one. If you find that stress overwhelms you on a daily basis, that you never have time to sit and relax, and sleep doesn't come easily, then you need to build in time to wind down. Be sensible—try taking a bath or shower at the end of the evening and then pray as you get into bed.

FIT
TIP

If you're feeling overstretched, give yourself a half hour tonight to relax completely.

RIGHT **It is important to relax and refresh your body as well as your mind.**

THE
HEALTHY SPIRIT

In order to keep your spirit as healthy as possible, you need to be open to what God's Spirit is offering you. For example, do you know what each of the fruits of the Spirit is? And are you aware of the purpose of spiritual gifts? How should His Spirit fit into your everyday life?

God commands all Christians to "…be filled with the Spirit." (*Ephesians 5: 18*). However, a lack of understanding often causes them to shy away from exploring what this means. Christians know about the mystery of the Trinity—three in one, God the Father, the Son, and the Holy Spirit—but do you know how you should relate to the Holy Spirit?

The Holy Spirit is a helper and counselor who God sent to earth after Jesus went back to heaven and He dwells in the heart of every Christian: "Having believed, you were marked in him with a seal, the promised Holy Spirit, who is a deposit guaranteeing our inheritance." (*Ephesians 1: 13–14*). He will be there to provide you with

"When he, the Spirit of truth, comes, he will guide you into all truth. He will not speak on his own; he will speak only what he hears, and he will tell you what is yet to come. He will bring glory to me by taking from what is mine and making it known to you."
John 16: 13–14

RIGHT **Giving yourself over to God completely will allow you to bear fruit as a Christian.**

BELOW LEFT **In order to keep your spirit healthy, you need to allow God's spirit to fill you daily.**

FIT
TIP

If there is a spiritual fruit you long for ask God to develop it more in your life.

power, strength, understanding, and guidance day by day if you allow Him to. He also speaks directly to your spirit, reminding you that you belong to God: "The Spirit himself testifies with our spirit that we are God's children." (*Romans 8: 16*). Therefore, in times of trouble or despair, you can look to Him to encourage you.

THE FRUIT OF THE SPIRIT

The Spirit bears fruit in your life when you submit yourself to God. *Galatians 5: 22–23* explains that, "…the fruit of the Spirit is love, joy, peace, patience, kindness, goodness, faithfulness, gentleness, and self-control… ." Each fruit changes your character to make it more holy, more like Jesus. These fruits display your growth and your maturity, and so they

> *"I am the vine; you are the branches. If a man remains in me and I in him, he will bear much fruit; apart from me you can do nothing."* John 15: 5

can be produced in ever-increasing quantities. They are important because "…they will keep you from being ineffective and unproductive in your knowledge of our Lord Jesus Christ." (*2 Peter 1: 8*).

When the fruit of the Spirit is evident in your life, this will be a clear demonstration to those around you that you belong to the Lord. You cannot produce the fruit for yourself, however hard you try. This means that if you want the fruit of the Spirit in your life then you need to be entwined with Him at all times.

THE FRUIT OF THE SPIRIT TEST

Love—Can I love people I don't naturally like?

Joy—Am I a happy Christian?

Peace—Am I at peace with myself, others, and God?

Patience—Am I able to be patient with those around me or do I find they exasperate me easily?

Kindness—Do I go out of my way to perform acts of kindness for those I come across day by day?

Goodness—Is my life characterized by doing good?

Faithfulness—Would I trust God whatever happens, whatever He allows to be done to me, or would I turn my back on Him if He did something I didn't like?

Gentleness—Do I confuse this with weakness?

Self-control—Is there any area of my life in which I lack self-control, either in my thoughts or elsewhere?

SPIRITUAL GIFTS

While the fruit of the Spirit changes your character, the gifts of the Spirit are designed to empower you for acts of service. God gives each person particular gifts in order to enable them to work effectively within the whole body of Christ (see Attend Church, *pages 30–31*). He says that: "Each one should use whatever gift he has received to serve others, faithfully administering God's grace in its various forms." (*1 Peter 4: 10*).

The gifts that are being referred to here include teaching, pastoring, hospitality, serving, prophesy, healing, wisdom, evangelism, encouragement, and giving, and they are specifically intended to build up the family of God.

Although it is certainly true that each person should evangelize, encourage their fellow Christians, and offer hospitality, the Bible makes it clear that some people have particular gifts in these areas.

"Now to each one the manifestation of the Spirit is given for the common good. To one there is given through the Spirit the message of wisdom, to another the message of knowledge by means of the same Spirit...to another gifts of healing by that same Spirit, to another miraculous powers... All these are the work of one and the same Spirit, and he gives them to each one, just as he determines."
1 Corinthians 12: 7–11

BELOW **You have particular gifts that make you an effective part of God's body.**

If you have read about spiritual gifts and are unsure what yours are, be reassured that the Holy Spirit has given you one or more. Your job is simply to discern what they are. Start by asking God to reveal your gifts; then take a look at what you enjoy doing the most. Consider the feedback you get from those you have served and look for signs that seem to affirm your abilities. Ask close Christian friends for an honest opinion on this issue, too. Continue to pray throughout the whole process. Once you know what your spiritual gifts are, all God asks is that you step out and use them faithfully.

NEVER GIVING UP

This book should have made you assess your spiritual life honestly, and it may have opened up some areas that you never thought existed before. Your life is a journey, and you are constantly developing. Now, you have some tools that will help keep your spirit healthy, you can go out and enjoy exploring your spiritual life to the fullest!

It's a good idea to keep this book on hand and work through the checkup every so often. You may find that the areas you most need to concentrate on change over time and this is a simple but effective way of pinpointing that.

The difficulties and pressures you encounter will vary, and you may find that an issue you thought you had dealt with effectively comes back months or even years later. Don't be disheartened. You are not alone in your struggles and remember that you should keep your final goal in sight at all times. Be assured that: "His divine power has given us everything we need for life and godliness through our knowledge of him who called us by his own glory and goodness." (2 Peter 1: 3).

> "Let us throw off everything that hinders and the sin that so entangles, and let us run with perseverance the race marked out for us." Hebrews 12: 1

Look to Jesus at all times because He, and He alone, is your spiritual lifeblood. His sacrifice has provided you with the strength and endurance you need to run your own particular race effectively. Therefore, discipline yourself to keep delving into His word, listening to Him, and pouring out your heart to Him. Keep in close fellowship with other Christians, also.

RIGHT **Keep your eyes focused on your goal and do everything you can to keep on track. During the hard times, remind yourself that you *will* complete the race.**

There will be times when you struggle and times when life is easier, but remember God is with you, urging you on at all times. Remember that He *has* provided you with everything you need.

LOOKING AHEAD

Now that you have worked through this book, can you see the specific things that have helped you advance along in your spiritual path? What are the things that you struggle with, that could cause you to slip back?

Ask yourself what you would you like to do with the rest of your life. Now what do you think God wants you to do with the rest of your life? How does your list compare or differ? On a separate piece of paper, list the six main things that you would like to see happen in your life, in the life of your family, and in the world at large. Now spend some time praying for all these things.

Remember, God has started a work in you and He won't give up until it is finished!

"He who began a good work in you will carry it on to completion until the day of Christ Jesus."
Philippians 1: 6

FURTHER READING

ARNOTT, John, *Importance of Forgiveness*, R. G. Mitchell Family Books, 1997.

BILLHEIMER, Paul, *Don't Waste Your Sorrows*, Bethany House, 1993.

GUMBEL, Nicky, *Questions of Life*, Kingsway Books, 2001.

KENDALL, R.T., *Total Forgiveness*, David C. Cook Publishing Company, 2002.

KENDRICK, Graham, *Learning to Worship as a Way of Life*, Bethany House, 1985.

LEA, Larry, *Learning the Joy of Prayer*, Kingsway Communications, 2001.

THOMAS, Jim, *Streetwise Spirituality*, Harvest House Publishers, 2001.

YANCEY, Philip, *Disappointment with God*, Zondervan Publishing House, 1987.

YANCEY, Philip, *Reaching for the Invisible God*, Zondervan Publishing House, 2002.

USEFUL WEB SITES

home.christianity.com—*site that offers Bible studies, teaching on theology and doctrine, and advice on how to share your faith.*

www.anchorlife.org—*learn more about God, His word, and how to pray at this site.*

www.cfdevotionals.org—*log onto this site daily to read "today's devotional." You can also browse the devotional archive by topic, date, and author (topics are various and include faith, fasting, humility, salvation, and stewardship).*

www.christianbasics.org—*a free online study course covering the basics of life as a Christian, such as the place of the Holy Spirit in your life and being part of a church etc.*

www.christianitytoday.com—*the online home of the magazine with the same name, this offers thought-provoking articles on varied subject matter.*

www.d-u-c-k-s.com—*d-u-c-k-s stands for "devoted unconditionally to Christ's kingdom and service." The site includes explanations of various Christian beliefs.*

www.gospelcom.net/spiritual_walk/—*includes studies, daily devotions, and articles to help you delve deeper into your faith.*

www.newhopenow.com—*includes articles on all aspects of the Christian life.*

www.sermons4u2.org—*great sermons online to browse for free.*

www.ucb.co.uk—*the Web site of the UK Christian radio. This also offers their "word for today" devotional readings online.*

INDEX

TAKING YOUR SPIRITUAL PULSE

ACKNOWLEDGMENTS

Thanks mum for all your support, hard work, and encouragement. And thanks Steve for being by my side throughout everything and for giving me inspiration—I couldn't have done this without you.

I would also like to thank all those at Palm Press who have helped make this book possible—Sophie Collins, John Hunt, Andrew Milne, and Caroline Earle.

All scripture quoted is the New International Version.

The Message *cover image, page 59: Copyright (c) by Eugene H. Peterson 1993, 1994, 1995, 1996, 2000, 20001, 2002. Used by permission of NavPress Publishing Group.*